GENERATIVE AI- WHAT & WHY?

DR DHEERAJ MEHROTRA

Copyright © Dr Dheeraj Mehrotra
All Rights Reserved.

This book has been self-published with all reasonable efforts taken to make the material error-free by the author. No part of this book shall be used, reproduced in any manner whatsoever without written permission from the author, except in the case of brief quotations embodied in critical articles and reviews.

The Author of this book is solely responsible and liable for its content including but not limited to the views, representations, descriptions, statements, information, opinions and references ["Content"]. The Content of this book shall not constitute or be construed or deemed to reflect the opinion or expression of the Publisher or Editor. Neither the Publisher nor Editor endorse or approve the Content of this book or guarantee the reliability, accuracy or completeness of the Content published herein and do not make any representations or warranties of any kind, express or implied, including but not limited to the implied warranties of merchantability, fitness for a particular purpose. The Publisher and Editor shall not be liable whatsoever for any errors, omissions, whether such errors or omissions result from negligence, accident, or any other cause or claims for loss or damages of any kind, including without limitation, indirect or consequential loss or damage arising out of use, inability to use, or about the reliability, accuracy or sufficiency of the information contained in this book.

Made with ♥ on the Notion Press Platform
www.notionpress.com

Contents

Preface

Generative AI, a growing subfield of artificial intelligence, promises to reinvent creativity and innovation. Generative AI bridges the gap between humans and machines in art, design, and beyond.

"Generative AI - What & Why?" explains this intriguing field to techies and laypeople. This book will examine Generative AI's complex algorithms, many uses, and future ramifications. Beyond the intricacies and rhetoric, it asks: Why should we care? Once we go further, readers will see that Generative AI isn't simply another tech term— a tool, collaborator, and inspiration. Generative AI challenges our vision of creativity in art, music, literature, design, and invention. Instead of competing, people and robots will work together.

Generative AI, like any robust technology, has drawbacks and ethical issues. The book will include expert perspectives, case studies, and thought experiments for a comprehensive understanding.

This book will encourage thinking, discussion, and innovation among AI researchers, students, and technology enthusiasts alike. We'll explore Generative AI's history, present, and future. Understanding precedes appreciation, they say. "Generative AI - What & Why?" will help people grasp this disruptive technology and imagine a boundless creative future. Welcome to a universe where man, machine, and muse blend. Start this fantastic adventure.

Warmly,

Dr Dheeraj Mehrotra

ONE

Introduction to Generative AI

An Overview of Generative Artificial Intelligence

A subfield within the huge terrain of artificial intelligence (AI) is swiftly gaining importance because of its potential to change several industries, ranging from the arts to engineering; this subfield is known as Generative AI. This subfield of artificial intelligence emphasises the production of original works, whether they take the form of a piece of music, a design, a piece of poetry, or even wholly new AI models. Diving into the foundations of Generative AI, its working, and its countless possibilities is vital to properly understanding its relevance and promise. This will allow you to comprehend both aspects fully.

Generative AI uses trained models to create new information, patterns, and solutions. Most standard AI systems analyze or interpret incoming data, whereas generative models create new material that matches training data.

The Generative Adversarial Network is the most well-known Generative AI architecture. Two neural networks—the Generator and the Discriminator—work together in GANs. The Generator generates data, whereas the Discriminator verifies it. The Generator wants to enhance its outputs so the Discriminator can't tell real from fake data. This adversarial process creates realistic material.

Generative AI has several uses:

GANs can generate convincing pictures and videos, including human faces and artwork.

Music Composition:

Generative models may learn musical patterns and compose new music in their style.

Text Generation:

GPT-3 generates cohesive, contextual text.

Molecular structure prediction for novel medications is possible using generative AI.

Design and Art:

Generative models help designers and artists create new works.

Generative AI has problems and ethical concerns, notably with content authenticity and the possibility for misleading or fraudulent material, such video deepfakes.

Establishment of the Generative AI

The concept of teaching computers to create material is fundamental to the field of generative artificial intelligence (AI). Unlike typical AI models, which make judgments based on the data fed into them (such as suggesting a song or locating an item in a picture), generative models take the process one step further. They come up with brand new, unique material due to the learning they do from massive quantities of data.

The Workings of Generative AI in Their Present Form

The Generative Adversarial Network, often known as a GAN, is now the most common method to fuel generative artificial intelligence. GANs comprise two types of neural networks: the Generator and the Discriminator. Ian Goodfellow first proposed them in 2014. They cooperate while simultaneously trying to outdo one another. The Discriminator is responsible for analysing the data produced by the Generator. The purpose of the Generator is to "trick" the Discriminator by gradually improving the realism of the data it produces over time. GANs can generate very lifelike outputs because of the continuous feedback loop that they use. These outputs may range from lifelike visuals to coherent passages of text.

Submissions as well as Accomplishments

The applications of generative artificial intelligence are as innovative as they are diverse:

Artists and designers use Generative artificial intelligence in the creative industries to create unique works of art and aid in the creation process. DeepDream is a program that was created by Google that alters photos by magnifying the qualities that are identified by neural networks. This results in the creation of strange art.

AI has been taught to write new compositions like great composers or even to develop entirely new genres of music. This ability has been applied to the field of music.

Generative AI plays an essential part in content creation, which includes a wide range of tasks, such as generating logical literature and the development of realistic settings for video games.

Drug development: By modelling molecular structures, Generative AI helps predict which chemicals may be prospective medications. This speeds up the tedious drug development process, which is currently done manually.

AI models can now forecast fashion trends and create new garments, opening the path for a merger of technology and haute couture. Fashion AI models can now predict fashion trends and even design new apparel.

Confrontations, as well as Ethical Implications

Although the prospects for Generative AI are enormous, the technology has difficulties. Training a GAN takes a substantial amount of computer power and a vast amount of data. Because of its high level of realism, the material that is created also raises ethical questions. Concerns about disinformation and privacy invasion have been raised in response to deepfakes, which are computer-generated videos that give the appearance of being shot in real life.

Furthermore, when robots begin to make works of art, music, and literature, problems about the nature of creativity and its validity are brought to the forefront. Is it possible for a machine to have creativity? Who is the owner of the rights to the artwork created by AI?

The Path That Lies Ahead

Even though it is still in its infant phases, generative artificial intelligence is developing at a breakneck speed. As technology advances, its incorporation into everyday activities will become less noticeable and more natural. Imagine a society in which artificial intelligence creates tailored clothing for you or a world in which personalised music tracks are generated on the spot for you.

Nevertheless, similar to any other robust technology, it is vital to use Generative AI responsibly. It is necessary to balance making the most of its potential and ensuring that ethical concerns are not overlooked.

The crossroads of technology and original thought is where generative AI finds its home. It symbolises how far we have gone in the field of artificial intelligence and a lighthouse pointing us toward a future rife with opportunities. The more we learn about and improve upon this technology, the more obvious it becomes that combining man and machine will push the limits of creativity, invention, and design in ways we are only starting to fathom.

TWO

Fundamental Principles and Components of Generative AI

In contrast to discriminative models, the generative approach to AI is a ground-breaking innovation in artificial intelligence. Generative models are focused on producing new material rather than categorizing or predicting labels based on the data that is inputted into them.

Their propensity for creation has been praised in various fields, including the arts, science, and technology. It is vital to master the fundamental ideas of Generative AI and its fundamental building blocks to comprehend it.

The Most Important Ideas Are:

Probabilistic Modeling: The goal of probabilistic modelling in generative artificial intelligence is to represent the probability distribution of the training data. After grasping this distribution, the AI can draw samples from it to generate new instances.

Adversarial Training: Generative models use adversarial processes, particularly GANs (Generative Adversarial Networks). A generator and a discriminator are the two models that "compete" against one another. While the discriminator determines whether or not the data is genuine, the generator produces new information, leading to an iterative improvement process.

Variability and Latent Space: Generative models map data points to a latent space, also known as a hidden space, which makes it possible for the created material to include variations and subtleties. Different outputs can be generated depending on how one moves through this area.

Reconstruction and Generation: Some generative models are trained to reconstruct input data, which enables them to learn efficient data representations. This allows the models to generate new data from existing data. After being taught, they can produce new material that is similar to the data that was supplied.

Principal Constituents:

In the context of GANs, the neural network responsible for producing material is called the generator. It begins with completely unpredictable noise and eventually improves its outputs as it undergoes training.

In picture production, for instance, the generator can start randomly creating pixel patterns. As the training continues, these patterns will begin to resemble real-world items or settings.

The discriminator is a partner to the generator in GANs and is responsible for determining whether the generated material is legitimate. It is important to recognize the difference between genuine data from the training set and fabricated data produced by the generator.

Example: When creating human faces, the discriminator examines the resulting picture to determine whether or not it exhibits inconsistencies and whether or not it seems to be a real human face.

Autoencoders are a neural network meant to encode and then decode the data sent into it. The data are represented more compactly thanks to the encoding, which also preserves its key characteristics. During the decoding process, the model will try to recreate the original data using this condensed form. Variational autoencoders, often known as VAEs, are extensions of autoencoders that provide generative capabilities by adding probabilistic characteristics.

An autoencoder, for instance, may be trained on several artworks. The encoder distils the core characteristics of each artwork into a condensed version, while the decoder works to produce the original work of art. After being taught, the decoder can produce visuals that resemble paintings.

RNNs stand for "recurrent neural networks." RNNs include memory cells that can record relationships inside sequences, which makes them particularly helpful for sequential data such as time series or text. They are useful for generating sequences, which may be done using generative tasks.

The following is an example of how an RNN trained in classical music compositions may produce new musical pieces while maintaining classical qualities.

Loss functions are mathematical functions that direct the training process. They are used to steer the process. When it comes to generative models, loss functions often include many terms. This helps ensure that the material produced is varied and of good quality.

Example: The loss function used in GANs considers how well the discriminator can tell the difference between genuine and false data and how effectively the generator can trick the discriminator.

Various Examples & Applications:

Image Synthesis:

GANs can generate various pictures, from human faces to artwork. StyleGAN, developed by NVIDIA, has created human faces that are so lifelike that they cannot be differentiated from actual ones.

Text Generation:

OpenAI's GPT models can create text that is not only coherent but also contextually relevant and even innovative.

Molecular Design:

Generative models may be used as a tool to assist in the process of building molecular structures for possible novel medications or materials.

Style Transfer:

The methods of neural style transfer allow for the creative style of one picture to be applied to the content of another image, resulting in astonishing visual effects.

Data Augmentation:

In situations with limited data, generative models can supplement datasets by producing additional synthetic instances. This is important for training strong machine learning models.

The capabilities of machines are being expanded thanks to advances in generative artificial intelligence (AI). One may get an appreciation for the potential and transformational influence that Generative AI might have across sectors by first comprehending the basic concepts and components of the technology. However, as with any other robust technology, deploying it with care and ethics is vital to guarantee its advantages are completely realized without resulting in unforeseen effects.

THREE

Risks in Generative AI

Risks in Generative AI

Although it is a wonder of modern technology and a demonstration of the progress made in artificial intelligence, generative AI is not without its potential drawbacks. The problems that these more complex systems bring become more challenging to solve and possibly more severe as their level of sophistication increases.

The following is an in-depth analysis of the dangers that are related with generative AI:

1. Deepfakes and misinformation: Generative models, particularly GANs, can create material that seems quite realistic but completely fabricated. This capability has produced what are known as "deepfakes," fake films or audios that are almost impossible to differentiate from the real thing. These fake news outlets can be used for harmful purposes, such as to propagate false information, smear persons, or interfere with political proceedings.

For instance, a film created to show a politician making a critical statement might be distributed to change public opinion or influence the results of elections.

2. Issues Relating to Intellectual Property Generative artificial intelligence has the potential to create works of music, art, narrative, or design aspects. This skill has the potential to challenge conventional perspectives on intellectual property. Who owns the copyright to music or a book if it was generated by a computer program? In addition, these technologies might be used to duplicate and redistribute information protected by intellectual property rights, raising concerns relating to piracy and plagiarism.

3. Economic Disruptions: Generative AI can design things, make art, write tales, or even write code, which means it can replace numerous positions that people typically perform. This might have a significant impact on the global economy. This might result in people losing their jobs or seeing upheavals in the labour market, which would need society to adapt to the new economic realities.

4. Loss of Trust: As the border between material created by AI and content made by humans continues to blur, consumers may begin to view digital content in general with scepticism. It is possible to cast doubt on the veracity of several things, including the validity of news sources, the sincerity of internet evaluations, and the trustworthiness of digital evidence presented in court.

5. Biased Outputs: Like all other AI models, generative models are only as good as the data they are trained on. This might lead to biased results. These models are susceptible to producing biased or stereotypical results if they are trained with biased data. This may contribute to perpetuating negative stereotypes or misrepresent the variety in the actual world.

An example of this would be a generative model trained mostly on pictures of male physicians and female nurses. This model would create images that reflect these biases, reinforcing age-old preconceptions.

6. The Generation of Unintended Information Generative artificial intelligence, particularly when it is automated, can potentially create indecent, offensive, or even hazardous information. Putting too much faith in automated processes devoid of human control might result in disastrous consequences for public relations.

7. A potential threat to information security is that generative AI might be utilised in cyberattacks. Imagine if AI systems can generate phishing emails that are precisely suited to particular targets and are thus practically impossible to differentiate from authentic correspondence. This could increase the hazards of cyber attacks to levels that have never been seen before.

8. Overdependence: Relying too much on generative artificial intelligence for content production may harm human creativity and innovation. The many patterns that make up human culture risk becoming less differentiated if businesses rely too much on computer programs when creating works of music, art, or design.

9. Ethical Implications of Generated Material: Generating material that accurately represents reality raises several severe ethical considerations. For example, using artificial intelligence to replicate the voice or likeness of someone who has passed away might be considered intrusive or insulting. In addition, artificial intelligence that generates information to emotionally manipulate consumers, such as by creating bogus endorsements or reviews, might result in ethical conundrums.

10. Environmental Impacts: Training generative models, particularly big ones, needs significant computer resources. Because of this, the expansion of such technology is a cause for worry from an environmental standpoint since it may result in significant carbon footprints.

The potency of generative artificial intelligence cannot be refuted; it provides a wide range of applications that have the potential to advance civilization. But with this power also comes the need to exercise extreme prudence. It is essential for governments, engineers, and society as a whole to be aware of these hazards and to work together to build frameworks that assure the appropriate and ethical use of generative artificial intelligence (AI). To fully realise the promise of generative AI while also mitigating the hazards that come with it, we will need to take preventative steps, conduct exhaustive research, and maintain a firm commitment to ethical principles.

FOUR

Understanding Prompt Injections, Hallucinations and Data Poisoning

The environment of artificial intelligence, particularly in deep learning and neural networks, is filled with various possibilities and difficulties. Several complexities determine the behaviour of AI models, with possible dangers arising from unexpected corners. Rapid injections, hallucinations, and data poisoning are examples of such complexities. An in-depth discussion of each topic is as follows:

1. Definition of Prompt Injections:

Prompt injections are when carefully prepared inputs (or prompts) are introduced into an artificial intelligence model to influence the model into generating the intended outputs. This is comparable to "feeding words" into a system to influence how it responds in a specific manner.

The implications are that it might be used maliciously in language models that depend largely on prompts. For instance, an attacker may utilize prompt injections to coerce the artificial intelligence into displaying prejudice, disseminating false information, or malfunctioning.

To mitigate this risk, it is vital to incorporate robustness tests for models, routinely test the system with various prompts, and create protections against fraudulent inputs.

2. Hallucinations:

Definition-

In artificial intelligence, "hallucinations" refers to situations where models create outputs that look reasonable but are not based on the actual world's input data or realities. These replies are effectively "made up" by artificial intelligence.

The repercussions include that it may be especially worrisome in decision-critical applications. For example, if a medical AI were to diagnose a patient based on a hallucination, this may have serious repercussions. In a similar vein, an AI model that is used to disseminate information can give information that is inaccurate or deceptive.

The prevalence of hallucinations may be mitigated by regularly refining and retraining models using various and accurate datasets in conjunction with human supervision. Providing people with the capacity to comprehend how the AI arrived at its decision is another advantage that may be gained by implementing model interpretability.

3. Data Poisoning:

Adding harmful data into a model's training set to distort the model's behaviour is called data poisoning. This kind of attack is strategic, and its objective is for the adversary to either quietly reduce the model's performance or create particular weaknesses. The implications stem from that neural networks, particularly deep learning models, rely on the training data they use. That tainted data may result in a wide variety of undesirable behaviours. For instance, a face recognition system that has been tampered with may be misled into misidentifying persons, and a recommendation system can be biased towards pushing certain material if it is manipulated correctly.

Maintaining vigilance throughout the data-gathering and preparation phases of mitigation is essential. Regular audits of the training data, discovering anomalies, and using reliable data sources may all be helpful. In addition, methods such as data sanitization may be used. This involves the detection and elimination of data points that are deemed to be anomalous or suspicious.

Concluding remarks:

It is becoming more critical to have a solid awareness of the possible dangers as the field of artificial intelligence (AI) continues to grow and touch more and more areas of society. Even though quick injections, hallucinations, and data poisoning only account for a small portion of the issues that AI faces, they highlight the need of thorough testing, ongoing learning, and ethical concerns in the deployment of AI. Researchers, developers, and consumers can only leverage the potential of AI responsibly and safely if they have a comprehensive knowledge of the problems that lie ahead.

Deep Dive Into Technical Matters:

Prompt Injections

The inference step of a model is taken advantage of by prompt injections. An attacker will painstakingly construct an input to bring about a desired outcome. The level of sensitivity to the initial cues may be particularly high for generative models, particularly those that use transformers such as the GPT series or BERT. For example, changing the wording of a query might result in different responses, even though the inquiry is looking for the same kind of information.

The actual world Take, for instance, chatbots, which are becoming more used in online customer care. If an adversary can understand the model's behaviour, they can structure their questions (prompts) to cause the bot to reveal information it is not meant to, which might result in a data breach.

Extended Mitigation Strategies:

Besides the already-stated remedies, one may also use adversarial training approaches. This kind of training involves the model being taught with a sequence of hostile prompts, strengthening its resistance to assaults of this nature.

Technical Deep Dive:

Hallucinations Most of the time, AI hallucinations are the consequence of overfitting, which is when the model is too aligned with its training data and cannot generalize well. When presented with unexpected inputs, the model may "hallucinate" outputs that look reasonable to it but are, in reality, erroneous or unconnected. This phenomenon is referred to as "paranoia."

The actual world Example: When using machine translation models, a statement may be translated into a grammatically accurate phrase but incorrect in context, thereby producing information lacking in the source text.

Extended Mitigation Strategies:

Techniques such as dropout, in which random neurons are "dropped" during training, may increase generalization and are examples of extended mitigation strategies. Combining the results of numerous models, Ensemble approaches might help reduce hallucinations.

The Dangerous Use of Data:

A Technical Deep Dive: Attacks that include data poisoning may be divided into targeted and non-targeted categories. During a targeted attack, data might be included that causes the model to produce certain harmful outputs when presented with certain inputs. The objective of an assault that is not targeted is for the attacker to reduce the overall performance of the model.

The actual world Consider the artificial intelligence of a vehicle that drives itself. If an adversary can access a vehicle's training data and corrupt it, they might create situations in which the vehicle incorrectly perceives stop signs, which could result in accidents.

Extended Mitigation Strategies: Differential privacy, a technique that guarantees individual data points do not unduly affect the result, may be used to lessen the effect of data poisoning. This strategy ensures that individual data points do not influence the conclusion. Active learning, in which the model chooses which data points it wants to learn from, may also be a solution since it can avoid potentially poisoned data by choosing which data points it wants to learn from.

The possible adversarial assaults and pitfalls in AI, such as prompt injections, hallucinations, and data poisoning, demonstrate why it is essential to take a defence-in-depth strategy when developing and deploying AI models. For example, prompt injections are an example of an adversary attack, while hallucinations and data poisoning are examples of a potential pitfall.

The promise of artificial intelligence is enormous; unfortunately, so is the possibility that it may be abused, either accidentally or on purpose. One must comprehensively grasp the technology and meticulously monitor its models to maximise artificial intelligence's advantages while mitigating potential drawbacks. The obligation of AI's stewards—its researchers, developers, and institutions—grows even more critical as the field of artificial intelligence becomes more entangled with our day-to-day lives.

FIVE

SECURITY IN GENERATIVE AI

Safety in Artificial Generative Intelligence

An interesting new facet has been added to the field of artificial intelligence with the advent of generative AI. This branch of AI can produce its own material, from visuals to writing. The potential uses are wide and imaginative, but they come with security problems that must be addressed. These concerns need to be addressed immediately. The term "security" in the context of generative AI refers to protecting both the models and the content created against harmful use. Additionally, it refers to protecting the data used and preventing any malicious manipulation of that data.

1. The threat landscape in generative artificial intelligence:

The proliferation of Generative Adversarial Networks (GANs) and models like as OpenAI's GPT series have created a Pandora's box of possible safety concerns, including the following:

Deepfakes are one of the most widely discussed security risks. Deepfakes entail using Generative AI to produce information that seems to be hyper-realistic but is, in fact, completely fake. This content may most often be found in video or voice recordings. These may be used to spread false information, commit fraud, or smear someone's reputation.

Integrity of the Data: Generative models can produce synthetic data. This data has the potential to contaminate actual datasets if it is accurately distinguished, which would help the quality and integrity of future models.

Model Manipulation Generative models may be susceptible to adversarial assaults, in which even minute changes to the model's input data can lead it to generate inaccurate outputs. These kinds of attacks are known as "model manipulation."

2. Ensuring the Safety of the Model:

Generative models, much like other types of AI models, need stringent safety precautions to be taken:

Training Models to Identify and Resist Adversarial Inputs One technique is to train models to identify and resist adversarial inputs. When adversarial instances are introduced while training, the model becomes more resilient and less likely to be tricked by malicious inputs.

Monitoring and Auditing: The continuous monitoring of the artificial intelligence model's inputs and outputs may aid in detecting unexpected patterns or anomalies, which might signal a breach in security or model drift. Auditing can also help in determining whether or not there has been a breach in security.

The interpretability of a model is essential because knowing why a model comes to a given conclusion may assist in determining whether or not the model is being used appropriately or influenced in some way.

3. Safeguarding the User-Generated Content:

The material that is generated by an AI system has to be protected, both in terms of establishing that it is genuine and preventing it from being used in inappropriate ways:

The process of embedding invisible watermarks is one method that may be used to validate the validity of the material that has been created. This might help trace the origin and confirm the legitimacy of the information.

Validation Tools: Using AI, tools may be designed to discriminate between actual material and content produced by AI. This assists in the early discovery of deep fakes and other forms of altered media.

4. Safeguards in Ethical and Legal Practices:

In addition to practical solutions, ethical and legal precautions are of the utmost importance:

Standards for Use:

Organizations that use generative AI should have crystal clear standards for using it ethically. These may include preventing the production of information that is damaging or deceptive and ensuring that there is openness about the usage of content created by artificial intelligence.

Legislation:

On a more global scale, governments and regulatory agencies throughout the globe are starting to adopt regulations surrounding the use of deepfakes and other AI-generated material to avoid its abuse, particularly in critical areas such as elections or the manipulation of public mood.

The risks to data security posed by generative AI are varied and constantly changing. Nevertheless, we can leverage the potential of generative AI while simultaneously limiting the hazards involved by using a mix of technological, ethical, and legal safeguards. The AI community, governments, and end-users must take the initiative to guarantee a secure and reliable AI-driven future.

SIX

Importance of Generative AI for Schools

The Significance of Generative AI for Educational Institutions

Introducing new technologies has brought about a dramatic shift in how education is delivered. Among all these technical advancements, Artificial Intelligence (AI) stands out as a forerunner in how contemporary education is developing. Artificial intelligence emphasising content generation, or Generative

AI, may provide enormous potential advantages to educational institutions.

Let's explore further the significance of generative artificial intelligence for academic institutions.

Generative artificial intelligence has the potential to develop instructional material that is suited to the specific requirements of each unique learner. Generative models can customize a student's study materials, quizzes, and assignments by considering the student's strengths, limitations, and preferred learning methods. This makes for a more efficient and personally relevant educational experience.

Learning a Language:

Generative AI has the potential to be an invaluable tool in the field of language teaching. Students will have an easier time grasping subtleties, idioms, and colloquialisms because of their ability to construct sentences in different languages that are correct from a grammatical standpoint. In addition, students working on their pronunciation and sentence structure may get real-time feedback from conversational AI.

Generative AI technologies may assist students in working on creative tasks such as writing, painting, music, or design. This can lead to enhanced creativity. Artificial intelligence can act as a digital muse for younger artists by generating storyline ideas for a tale, creating virtual artworks, or even composing unique music.

Visualizations and Simulations:

With visual aids, it is much simpler to grasp complex topics, which is particularly helpful in fields such as physics, chemistry, and biology. Students having difficulty visualizing abstract concepts or occurrences difficult to recreate in a classroom context may benefit from using generative artificial intelligence, which can create realistic simulations and 3D models.

Tutoring & Assistance:

Chatbots powered by generative AI have the potential to act as tutors around the clock, responding to questions posed by students even when school is not in session. They can walk students through difficult difficulties, provide explanations, and even recommend extra resources that students may use to enhance their education.

Feedback Provision:

Due to high class sizes, teachers often feel it is tough to deliver timely feedback to their students. Generative artificial intelligence (AI) may help instructors by automatically evaluating assignments and offering constructive comments. This frees teachers to concentrate on more qualitative parts of the classroom experience.

Generative artificial intelligence has the potential to develop educational material that is individualized for pupils who have specific requirements. For instance, creating study materials in formats such as braille, sign language, or simplified English may accommodate a greater variety of student's individual learning needs, guaranteeing that no student is left behind.

Future Readiness:

As artificial intelligence (AI) becomes more prevalent in various fields, the incorporation of generative AI in educational settings guarantees that students are acquainted with these technologies, preparing them for future vocations and cultivating a generation skilled at maximizing the potential of AI.

In addition to assisting students in their academic pursuits, generative AI may make administrative work more efficient. For instance, it may develop schedules, optimize the distribution of resources, and even prepare messages for parents, all of which contribute to a more streamlined school running.

A Culture of Innovation is Fostered by Research Senior students or individuals working on research projects may use Generative AI tools to analyze enormous datasets, develop hypotheses, or even construct prototypes, which helps to promote a culture of innovation and encourages research.

Using generative artificial intelligence (AI) in educational institutions is a step toward modernity and redefining education delivery. This opens the way for a learning environment that is more individualized, interesting, and effective for the learner. Concerns around ethics and data protection and the possibility of becoming too reliant on technology are the difficulties that must be considered.

Generative AI, however, offers the possibility of dramatically upgrading the educational environment, which would benefit both educators and students, provided that it is implemented correctly and approached in a balanced manner.

SEVEN

MULTIPLE TYPE QUESTIONS ON GENERATIVE AI

1. Which of the following is a popular Generative AI model?
   a) CNN (Convolutional Neural Network)
   b) RNN (Recurrent Neural Network)
   c) GAN (Generative Adversarial Network)
   d) SVM (Support Vector Machine)

Answer: c) GAN (Generative Adversarial Network)

2. What are the two main components of a GAN?
   a) Generator & Discriminator
   b) Predictor & Optimizer
   c) Encoder & Decoder
   d) Forward & Backward Propagation

Answer: a) Generator & Discriminator

3. Which of the following is NOT a typical use case for Generative AI?
   a) Image generation
   b) Text summarization

c) Data augmentation

d) Content recommendation

Answer: d) Content recommendation

4. VAEs, which are also used in generative AI, stand for:

a) Variable AutoEncoders

b) Versatile Algorithmic Entities

c) Vision-Associated Experiments

d) Variational AutoEncoders

Answer: d) Variational AutoEncoders

5.In a GAN, the main job of the discriminator is to:

a) Generate data samples

b) Reduce model loss

c) Distinguish between real and fake data samples

d) Encode input data

Answer: c) Distinguish between real and fake data samples

6. Which of the following is a primary challenge in training GANs?

a) Mode collapse

b) Underfitting

c) Bias-variance trade-off

d) Gradient ascent

Answer: a) Mode collapse

7. Generative AI models primarily learn through which of the following?

a) Supervised learning

b) Reinforcement learning

c) Unsupervised learning

d) Transfer learning

Answer: c) Unsupervised learning

8. Which of the following AI models can be used for text-based generative tasks?

a) CNN

b) GAN

c) Transformer models

d) AutoEncoders

Answer: c) Transformer models

9. Deepfake technology often utilizes:

a) GANs

b) Decision Trees

c) Linear Regression

d) k-Nearest Neighbors

Answer: a) GANs

10. In a GAN, when the generator gets better at generating fake samples, the discriminator's task becomes:

a) Easier

b) More complex

c) Remains the same

d) Irrelevant

Answer: b) More complex

11. Which one among the following is not primarily a generative model?

a) Restricted Boltzmann Machine (RBM)

b) GAN

c) Variational Autoencoder (VAE)

d) Residual Neural Network (ResNet)

Answer: d) Residual Neural Network (ResNet)

12. The 'latent space' in Generative AI refers to:

a) The space where all generated data resides

b) The underlying structure of a dataset represented in lower dimensions

c) The area where the discriminator operates

d) The final output layer of the generator

Answer: b) The underlying structure of a dataset represented in lower dimensions

13. Which of these challenges does Generative AI pose in terms of content authenticity?

a) Deepfakes
b) Data compression
c) Overfitting
d) Stochastic gradient descent
Answer: a) Deepfakes

14. In GANs, the term 'adversarial' refers to:
a) The competitive process between the generator and discriminator
b) The external adversarial attacks on the model
c) The adversarial learning rate
d) The type of data used for training
Answer: a) The competitive process between the generator and discriminator

15. In VAEs, what do they try to optimize in addition to the reconstruction loss?
a) Generative loss
b) Latent loss
c) Adversarial loss
d) Discriminative loss
Answer: b) Latent loss

16. Generative AI models can be used for:
a) Data synthesis
b) Classification
c) Regression analysis
d) Time-series forecasting
Answer: a) Data synthesis

17. What is the primary goal of the generator in a GAN?
a) To improve its ability to generate data that the discriminator can't differentiate from real data
b) To correctly classify real vs. generated data
c) To minimize the generative loss
d) To improve the efficiency of the neural network

Answer: a) To improve its ability to generate data that the discriminator can't differentiate from real data

18. Which of these is an advantage of using generative AI?

a) Fixed dataset size

b) Data augmentation

c) Improved classification

d) Reduced computational power

Answer: b) Data augmentation

19. StyleGAN, a popular generative model, is primarily used for:

a) Text synthesis

b) Image synthesis

c) Audio synthesis

d) Video synthesis

Answer: b) Image synthesis

20. Which of these is a potential real-world application of Generative AI?

a) Optimizing server loads

b) Predicting weather

c) Generating artwork

d) Natural Language Processing (NLP) tools

Answer: c) Generating artwork

21. What is the most common metric used to evaluate the quality of generated samples in GANs?

a) Precision

b) Recall

c) Inception score

d) F1 score

Answer: c) Inception score

22. Why might a GAN fail to converge during training?

a) The generator is too accurate

b) The discriminator is perfectly classifying data

c) The learning rate is too low
d) All of the above
Answer: d) All of the above

23. Which of these is a limitation of GANs?
a) They cannot generate high-resolution images
b) They can be difficult to train
c) They are inefficient in data augmentation
d) They cannot operate on GPUs
Answer: b) They can be difficult to train

24. Which model would you typically use for generating sequences of text?
a) CNN
b) LSTM
c) GAN
d) VAE
Answer: b) LSTM

25. Which of the following scenarios can benefit from Generative AI?
a) Creating virtual environments for game development
b) Detecting credit card fraud
c) Power grid optimization
d) Web scraping
Answer: a) Creating virtual environments for game development

About The Author

Dheeraj Mehrotra, MS, MPhil, PhD (Education Management)., a white and a yellow belt in SIX SIGMA, a Certified NLP Business Diploma holder, is an Educational Innovator, Author, with expertise in Six Sigma In Education, Academic Audits, Neuro-Linguistic Programming (NLP), Total Quality Management In Education, an Experiential Educator, a CBSE Resource towards School Assessment (SQAA), CCE, JIT, Five S, and KAIZEN. He has authored over 100 books on topics which include Computer Science, AI, Digital Body Language, NLP, Quality Circles, School Management, Classroom Effectiveness and Safety and Security in schools. A former Principal at De Indian Public School, New Delhi, (INDIA), NPS International School, Guwahati, and Education Officer at GEMS, Gurgaon, with an ample teaching experience of over Two Decades, he is a certified Trainer for Quality Circles/ TQM in Education and QCI Standards for School Accreditation/ School Audits and Management. He has also been honoured with the President of India's National Teacher Award in the year 2006 and the Best Science Teacher State Award (By the Ministry of Science and Technology, State of UP), Innovation in Education for his inception of Six Sigma In Education by Education Watch, New Delhi and Education World- Best Teacher Award, BOLT Learner Teacher Award by Air India, 'Innovation in Education Award 2016' by Higher Education Forum (HEF), Gujarat Chapter, among others. He has developed over 150 FREE EDUCATIONAL MOBILE Apps for the Google Play Store exclusively for Teachers, Students, and Parents. This work has been recognised by the LIMCA

BOOK OF RECORDS & INDIA BOOK OF RECORDS as the only Indian to draw that feast. Dr Mehrotra is a PRINCIPAL at KUNWARS GLOBAL SCHOOL, Lucknow, India. He has conducted over 1000 workshops globally on "Excellence In Education" integrated with Total Quality Management and Six Sigma, Technology Integration in Education (TIE), Developing towards being ROCKSTAR TEACHERS, including Cyberspace, Cyber Security, Classroom Management, School Leadership & Management, and Innovative teaching within classrooms via Mind Maps, NLP and Experiential Learning in Academics. He is an active TEDx speaker and can be viewed on the YouTube TEDx channel. As a premium UDEMY Instructor, he has developed over 450 courses and caters to over 8 Lakh students from 180 countries. He can be visited at www.authordheerajmehrotra.com

Books By The Same Author

PROMPT
ENGINEERING
THE GAME-CHANGING
SKILL YOU NEED TO
MASTER IN 2023!
UNDERSTANDING
Prompt
Engineering
Dr Dheeraj Mehrotra
NOW AVAILABLE AT
amazon

UNDERSTANDING
DATA SCIENCE
Dr Dheeraj Mehrotra

It is worth knowing now!
digital
body
Language
Dr Dheeraj Mehrotra

99.99% know
about ChatGPT
but only 0.01%
know how to use it
NOW AVAILABLE AT
amazon
Understanding
ChatGPT
Dr Dheeraj Mehrotra
@199/- Only.

www.ingramcontent.com/pod-product-compliance
Lightning Source LLC
LaVergne TN
LVHW040953150826
845672LV00002B/684

9798891334960